POKER: A WOMAN'S GAME

Lafaya Mitchell, LMFT

A Ray of Light Publishing

Contents

Title Page

Copyright

Foreword

Poker Slang Glossary

Introduction

Poker: Is This a Woman's Sport? — 1

Wisdom from Some Power-Hitting Ladies in Poker — 17

Badass Women in Poker — 20

Only the Strong Survive — 29

The Lafaya Way — 34

Poker Couples: The Good, The Bad, and The Ugly — 47

Poker, Gambling and Addiction — 54

Self-Care is Important to Winning in Poker — 59

It Ain't the Dealer's /Donkey's Fault?? — 63

Poker is a SICK SICK game — 67

Surviving Red Alert Brain   71

Poker PTSD   78

Instincts, It Stinks   80

Other Feelings   84

About The Author   89

Books By This Author   91

Foreword

by

James N. Mitchell

Lafaya Annette Mitchell is a very complex and confusing human being. She always seems to do and be the opposite of what people looking from the outside would expect. People often don't know what to make of her. She could sit at the poker table, super focused with headphones on and look like the meanest black girl in the world; I know she's concentrating, other people think she's mean as hell. OR her infectious playful side is out to play. When she's in that mode everybody can hear and see it. You can't miss her great big beautiful smile that lights up her face and the entire room, with a great big laugh to match. It's impossible to miss either one; no matter where I am in the poker room; I can pinpoint her vicinity.

The first time I saw her was when she walked into my local home casino, she bought into our 4-8 limit Texas Holdem game for $40 and whooped ass. She had no idea what she was doing; the other players had to tell her what to bet and how much it took to raise almost every hand. But that didn't matter. She was running hotter than fish grease. That girl could not lose. At one point, a hand played out in which by the river having a 10 in your hand would give you a one card straight. One of the old guys at the table said to Lafaya, "Show em the 10 baby." She flipped over the 10 which pissed off the other guys she beat in the hand because she called all the way to the river without any good draw. Me and the old guys laughed heartily. I figured out quickly to just stay out of her way. She was on a heater. She left with over $400!

Eventually, she started hanging out at our local card room frequently. We started to get to know each other a little better and then she started asking me questions about how to play poker. I must admit that I was super hesitant to answer her questions at first because she seemed to be kind of intelligent and I didn't want to give away too much information. Our mentor/mentee relationship eventually deepened into intimate feelings, and we started dating.

I remember being SHOCKED by her reaching onto my plate of food on our FIRST date and grabbing the food she thought looked good off MY plate. My initial thought was, "What in the world is wrong with this chick?" I learned later that she LOVES to throw people off guard and get a reaction out of them. She gets some kind of thrill out of it. I'm sure you will be shocked more than a few times reading some of her inner thought rantings in this book.

I also remember her cussing players and the dealers out at the poker table back in the day and thinking, "What is wrong with this chick?" One time, we met up and played some basketball at a local park. She decided to show up early with her son and get some practice in. She wound up tearing her ACL and tried to play through the pain! Again I wondered, "What is wrong with this chick?"

She hated losing so much, it was painful just playing poker with her at home for fun. Or chess. Or Yahtzee. Or any game for that matter. She may throw the whole deck of cards or flip the board game over just because she lost! But, as I got to know her, it was quickly very clear to me that this strange black girl therapist with long dreadlocked hair who listens to all kinds of music from rap to rock and starts dancing to any music, including music in commercials, had a well-hidden heart of gold.

One day she just flat-out 'kidnapped' (man-napped) me and took me to what became my new home. We have been virtually inseparable since. Lafaya (Fay) and I spend almost all of our time together. I have been with this strong, complex, sometimes crazy woman for over 15 years and counting! We have both learned a lot together, and have grown to be better partners through the experiences we have persevered through.

Now enough about us. What qualifies this, in

times past, certifiably nutty woman to teach anybody anything about the mental game? First and foremost, Lafaya has personally mastered managing her own mental health. You'll find a lot about her process from crazy to calm in this book. Through her profession (Masters-level mental health therapist) she has figured out a way to teach others to do the same. Her work with hypersensitive children and their families became so well received that she was asked to write books explaining to parents and colleagues how she gets such good results with children others would write-off as 'impossible to engage.' She has published three parenting books and created a training curriculum on her philosophy, "The Lafaya Way." She has taught her curriculum to several groups of overwhelmed parents and multiple non-profits working with children living with autism, suffering from severe ADHD, and those coping with Intergenerational Trauma.

After receiving some mental game of poker coaching herself, Lafaya quickly recognized that "The Lafaya Way 4 Core Steps" could very much apply for what was needed for her to calm down at the poker table.

Both life and poker can have their tough days. Nobody can win tournaments all the time and we are not handed happiness easily in life. Having Lafaya's tool bag of tips and tricks to help navigate tough days and moments strengthens your poker

All in for his tournament life, James Mitchell turns over JJ and has run in to the AA of Thomas Haury.

mental game AND how you deal with difficult life circumstances. I should know this best; she is my wife! I have learned from Lafaya MANY tips that have improved my mental game, my parenting skills, and my overall perspective on challenges... I, myself, use several techniques taught in this book every time I sit at the poker table, at home dealing with our three adult- and three adopted children, as well as at work, dealing with frustrating work-related situations. They are the keys I have identified as most important for my own poker success and success in living a happy life.

Lafaya has a special way of entertaining, surprising, and teaching, all at the same time. All I can say is you'll learn a lot. And enjoy the ride, because she is no-holds barred in this book. If you're allergic to cuss words, step away, this book is not for you. It's time to jump on the crazy train and take a ride!

James Mitchell
Dec 3, 2024

Poker Slang Glossary

You don't need to know Poker to get a lot out of this book. Even so, this Poker Slang Glossary might come in handy as you waltz through several nightmare hands with our intrepid author, Lafaya Mitchell. The four-letter words are self-explanatory, the rest are defined, below.

-ED., Lonnee Rey

Baby flush- A poker hand that contains five cards of the same suit; the player's hole cards are typically very low cards (seven and under.)

Bad Beat- When a clearly inferior hand beats a dominating hand (i.e. Pocket Queens beats Pocket Aces)

Big Blind- The second player to the left of the button required to place a mandatory bet before the players see their cards

Blinds- Mandatory bets made before a hand begins that establish the stakes for entering the hand.

Bluff- A bet or raise made with a weaker hand to trick opponents into folding their stronger hands

Bubble- A crucial moment in a poker tournament when the next player to be eliminated will not win any money. The remaining players will receive their share of the winnings (in the money)

Bubble Vote- Sometimes when there is one player left to be eliminated before everyone else is in the money, the players are asked if they would like to vote to allow a portion of the winnings to be allotted to everyone currently left in the tournament. The prospective bubble shares in the winnings too.

Button/Dealer Button- A marker that indicates the player who is acting last in a deal. The button is considered the most advantageous position to be in because the player can see what other players have decided to do before they must act. The button moves around the table with each betting round.

Call- Matching the amount bet by another player to stay in the hand

Cutoff- One of poker's late position; the position before the button

Donkey/Donk- A player who plays poorly or makes bad decisions, often losing money as a result. However, sometimes they get really lucky and give "bad beats"

Double Bubble- When there are two spots until everyone else splits their share of the winnings and two players are knocked out at the same time.

Flop- The first three of five community cards dealt face-up in the center of the table after the initial round of betting. The flop is a significant event in a poker hand because it determines which players can make a winning hand by combining their hole cards with the community cards

Game Theory Optimal (GTO)- A poker strategy that involves making decisions based on a set of variables and cards to maximize long-term profit. The goal of GTO poker is to become and unexploitable opponent and improve your chances of winning

Hole cards- Each player at the poker table receives two cards face down

LearnWPT- The official poker training platform of the World Poker Tour (WPT)

Non-robots- People more inclined to show feeling and emotions

Pre-flop- The period before the flop is dealt, when players are dealt their hole cards and betting begins

Raise- When a player increases the highest bet

River- After the turn, a final card is dealt face up with the community cards (the 5th and last card)

Shove- Going all-in; a player puts all of their chips in the pot

Small Blind-   The first player to the left of the "button"; typically required to pay half the minimum bet for the table up front

Suck Out- A player drawing out on an opponent to win a hand after having been an underdog to do so

Tanking- Taking a lot of time to make a decision on what action to take

The Floor- A casino employee who acts as a referee at the poker table, responsible for resolving disputes, enforcing the rules of the game, and overseeing fair play at the poker table

Turn- After the flop, a single card is dealt face-up with the community cards (the 4th card)

Introduction

by

Lafaya Mitchell

L et me start by saying, if you don't like this black female being at the poker table, and you think I should have my stereotypically dumb ass at home tending to my kids and cooking a meal, FUCK YOU!

The level of Bitch-asm that you deal with as a female poker player is relentless. The bottom level bastards that have fucked with me at the poker table over the years only drove me to want to be a better player; so, thank you very fucking much!

There are plenty of people that don't want to see us at the table. However, as is with racism, sexism has become increasingly more masked, but subtly apparent. (Seriously, sometimes not even that subtle.)

I have run into situations where groups of 4-5 guys would pile into every hand I would play, just to try to knock me out. I used to get extremely angry at the table, feeling victimized by these donkey-holes.

However, none of the haterism, sexism, racism, bad calls, bad beats and bad cards really matter over the long run. In life, there is adversity. It doesn't matter what direction it comes from nor how it manifests itself; all humans experience it.

The goal is to learn how to rise above; learn from and thrive through adversity. For me (and I'm sure you as well, if you're reading this), that means figuring out why shit bothers me so much.

The honest truth is other people's shit is their shit and taking their shit on is a choice. I always say to my therapy clients [yes, my crazy ass is a therapist], "Imagine if someone walked up to you holding a pile of shit in their hands and said 'Here take this,' trying to place it in your hands. Would you take that shit or let it drop on the ground?" Even though this is a gross analogy, it's very fitting for life, don't you think? If we could master not taking other people's shit from them, literally and figuratively, our existence would be exponentially cleaner and more peaceful.

As a point of fact, I have enough of my own shit, that's all mine, to deal with. I don't have time nor space for other people's crap. Alas, learning "not to personalize," as one of my favorite all time philosophers Don Miguel Ruiz suggests in his book, "The Four Agreements," is one of the single most difficult things to do in life. As with anything else though, with knowledge and practice, we can get better and better at not personalizing or "taking on other people's fists full of shit."

To help out with the 'gaining knowledge area,' I'll be presenting to you the method I've used for over 20 years that has helped me to be consistently successful in my work with those experiencing what I call "Red Alert Brain" or crisis mode. During crisis mode our baser instincts take over and we are typically operating from our animal (emotional) brain as opposed to our frontal lobe (logic.) We tend to call being in red alert mode while playing poker, *going on tilt,* or, as I like to call it: T.I.L.T.-Temporary Interruption in Logical Thinking.

Whether the cause is nature or nurture (biology or circumstance), all humans experience "Red Alert Brain" at one time or another. Those of us who struggle with emotional regulation (hypersensitivity) enter quite a bit more easily into Red Alert Brain. Have you ever seen a person have a complete meltdown and did not quite understand why they would become so upset over something most people would deem unimportant? You were more than likely witnessing the effects of Red Alert Brain activation in a hypersensitive individual.

The philosophy I'll be introducing to you, "The Lafaya Way," was developed in 2016 because of the demand by the parents, organizations, and colleagues I worked with to share the innovative strategies I used to successfully work with hypersensitive children/teens/adults who failed to improve in every program they would try ... until they got to me. I took on the challenge and was able to take what I thought was just a gift for breakthrough and put it into a philosophy containing four tangible steps to success. I was able to create a curriculum to teach to others which helped them achieve better results with difficult-to-reach hypersensitive individuals.

A few years after launching The Lafaya Way, I was blessed with an opportunity to have a session with one of the best Mental Game thinkers in the world, World Poker Tour (WPT) affiliate, Jared Tendler (thank you LearnWPT.) During our session, it became quite clear to me that what I teach my hypersensitive clients is very fitting for dealing with the mental side of poker, especially when it comes to battling T.I.L.T.

I started to take what I call my "4 Core Steps" and put them to practice as a way to combat my tendency to go on FULL TILT. Before working my steps, I would go on tilt and blow up about almost every unfair thing about the game so often that my husband would tell me, in the nicest way he could, that poker might not be the game for me. Seriously, the fits that I would have were just plain embarrassing.

The combination of the GTO (Game Theory

Optimal) strategies I learned through LearnWPT and working The Lafaya Way 4 Steps, (calming my tendency to go into instant red alert mode constantly), leveled my game up exponentially. After about 10 solid years of playing poker badly, I could finally compete. Before, I would just take a molly-whopping dang near every time I sat at the table; now, I'm a bit of a force to be reckoned with.

Journey with me as I lead my fellow non-robots into incrementally better success over time by sharing a phenomenal pathway to maintaining cooler internal systems in the extremely high pressure, stress-inducing game of poker. Are you in? Cause I'm all-in.

Poker: Is This A Woman's Sport?

T he first time I saw poker was in 2006 on ESPN . My ex-husband started watching lots of football on ESPN because his cousin had gone pro and earned a spot on the New Orleans Saints football team. One day, the TV was white-noising like it was often left to do, and I looked up to see a bunch of guys of all ages, sizes, and fitness levels sitting around a table playing cards.

Being a very competitive basketball player back in the day, I was personally offended by the fact that this no athletic ability required card game was being passed off as a sport.

I specifically said, "How in the hell is this crap supposed to be a sport?" I had no idea that it was possible for a card game

to be a sport. The only card games I had ever played were spades, speed, slap jack, go fish, blackjack and "I declare war." I scowled at the television, as if the people in charge of putting that junk on TV could see me, immediately snatched up the remote, whipped my hand around like a composer waving his stick to conduct a symphony, and turned to a different channel.

Some time later there the TV was again, left on the sports channel and I heard words that sounded familiar to me. One of the poker game announcers (it was World Series of Poker- WSOP, but I didn't know that back then) said, and I'm ad libbing,"He made a straight to beat other dude's three of a kind. The terms "straight" and "three of a kind" immediately caught my attention because I LOVE the game of Yahtzee; that game is my jam! Hearing terms used from a game that I loved stirred up a strong curiosity in me and I wondered, 'What's this game all about anyway?' So, I started watching it; picked up on the fact that there was a psychological component to this game and instantly fell in love with it.

In order to learn how to play poker, I clearly had to do some research because not all of the hands made matched exactly to Yahtzee. There was no Yahtzee (five of a kind) in this poker game they called Texas Holdem. In addition, I was 31 years old and my only exposure to poker had been maybe catching a glimpse of men around the table playing it in a cowboy movie. The beautiful ladies were either sitting on the men's laps or serving them drinks. Honestly, I hadn't really seen any women yet on the

ESPN channel playing poker, either. I had not yet been introduced to the magnificent wonder, Vanessa Selbst. But, I didn't need any female examples; I've always been a firm believer that anything men can do I can do better.

After a bit of research, I became OBSESSED with Texas Holdem and did not care for any of the other versions of poker. I initially had no place to practice all of the very basic stuff I was learning about the game. So, I decided I'd make the game part of my work as a therapist. I mostly worked with kids on the Autism spectrum at the time and "play therapy" was a big part of what I did to help them build social skills. Playing poker at work with the kids, using candy and tokens to make our bets, was a huge hit. They would open up quite a bit more through the game, helping me to achieve therapeutic objectives more quickly while I practiced playing poker myself. I was on cloud nine because Lafaya LOVES multi-tasking!

After watching poker on TV, and practicing with my clients for about a year, I decided it was time to visit a small little hole in the wall casino with "Texas Holdem" written on the bottom portion of their sign. That little white sign in a small shopping center with only a liquor store, a bar, and a small casino, constantly caught my attention; it reeled me in like a prize fish.

One day, I finally braved going into the little casino.

In case there was something scary about the place, my ex-husband was in tow. We were greeted by a short Latino guy, who I later learned was the owner of that fine establishment. He asked me what my name was; I had to think quickly because my name, Lafaya, sounds just like the Spanish words la fea, meaning "ugly girl" in Spanish. I told him my name was Fay, and that name has basically stuck with me. Most of my friends in the poker world call me Fay. I didn't know this at the time, but the name Fay also gave me a bit of a clear separation between my "real" world and my mysterious poker playing world. I mean really, what sense does it make for a therapist to get involved in a world of gambling??

Anywho, I nervously walked into that casino with exactly $100. I had no intention of losing a bunch of money trying to play a game. I let the little Latino guy know I wanted to play Texas Holdem. He escorted me over to the table in their far left corner, a $4-$8 limit game. He said that the minimum to play was $40. I was ELATED to hear that I didn't even have to use my whole $100 to play. LET'S GOOOO!

I sat down to play and didn't know what the hell I was doing. The betting patterns were confusing so I just put out whatever amount they told me I was supposed to. BUT, I had some SERIOUS beginner's luck. I could not lose a hand. It didn't matter what hand I played, I won. I accumulated $400 and left, taking no chances of giving it back. Of course, after that I was HOOKED. That place became my great escape from a not-so-happy home life; my second home.

I met my current husband, James, at that little hole in the wall. He was actually at the table with me the first day I visited. I do not remember seeing him then because I was hyper-focused on trying to figure out how to bet and stack all of those chips that kept flowing my way at such a fast pace. James did not start out in a good place on my radar. He was a REALLY GOOD player that whooped ass on the daily and after that lucky Day One, I was the fish. He would kick my butt constantly, playing his strategically sound hands that I understood NOTHING about. I had no idea how much there was to learn in order to really compete in poker. I thought he was picking on me because I was black, assuming his bald-headed, blue eyed, blond eyebrows-having ass was some type of racist skinhead or something. I could not stand him and wanted to get better at the game so that I could serve up a few ass kickings to him myself.

Of course, my initial evaluation of him was so WRONG I can't even express it strongly enough in text. I hadn't had the chance to hear him say much at the table because he would sit there with his dark sunglasses and hoodie on silently assassinating players and collecting chips. His nickname at that place was literally the Unibomber. As my frequency of visits to the little casino up-ticked to daily, I finally got a chance to see James in his social habitat.

His best friends were these Black and Latino dudes, which immediately dispelled the myth that he was a complete racist. Then I heard him speak. There was this cool twang in his voice and something very interesting about his tone. I later learned he was born in New Orleans. I could tell by his conversation that he was clearly intelligent, quite a bit more so than many of the people in that place. He immediately became a person of interest on my radar.

I had no romantic interest in him at the time because, first of all, he was not anything like what I would consider my type. I mean, if I was going to go white boy, he could at least have some kind of darker features, right? I did, however, decide that this man was the smartest person in the room *and* the best poker player, so he's going to teach me how to play poker the right way. I started out by asking him little probing questions about his play. I could tell he was hesitant to answer, but he couldn't resist answering my charming self. It advanced to my constantly checking in with him about hands. He became a bit of a coach or mentor to me. I started whooping a lot more ass in poker and he would come behind me telling other players, "I taught her everything she knows." They would get upset and say "No you didn't." I would chime in, replying, "Yes, he did; he's my Sensei." This was the beginning of a BEAUTIFUL friendship.

After about a year or two, I experienced what I considered such a bad beat by a donk holding 2-5 of spades, I tried to swear off poker. I think I said something like "Fuck this fake ass game; I'm not wasting my time playing this game anymore!" I was determined to stay away from that stupid little casino, and was successful with that goal for about six months. I did not miss going to the casino much because I had replaced my time there by going to Bingo with my sister, and still got to play Holdem with my clients. I did, however, miss Tallboy (this is what I used to call James before I could remember his name.) I would drive by the little casino, neck outstretched, searching hard to see if I could catch a glimpse of my now cool friend, Tallboy, from the road.

One day I thought to myself, 'Just drive through the little shopping center to see if you can see him to at least tell him hi.' I drove through and sure enough, there he was having a cigarette in the front of the casino. I walked up to him to say hey and gave him the first hug we'd ever given to each other. It felt quite natural to give him a hug since I hadn't seen him in such a long time. I noticed for the first time how really TALL and SKINNY he was during this hug. My head fit somewhere near the bottom of his chest and his waist was so small that I felt like I was able to hug myself and him at the same time. When I asked, he told me he was 6 foot 5-inches tall. I wondered how in the world I missed this because I have a bit of a tall fetish. Anyway, after opening the gates, hugging became something we did every day. Yes, I started frequenting the little casino again. It was REALLY nice to be around my friend again, with the added benefit of playing poker, which I loved. Bingo SUCKS!

By this time, my marriage had virtually deteriorated into pending divorce, while Tallboy and I had grown exponentially closer. After a while, I started to realize that I liked his hugs a little bit too much. I would hug him and linger. It felt safe and comfortable there and he smelled REALLY GOOD! Eventually, my marriage ended and I decided to pursue James.

I behaved very much like a high school girl in my pursuit, sometimes touching my leg to his while we were sitting down just to see if he would let our legs touch for a while, a sure sign that he liked me back. When he didn't move his leg, it was on. I asked him out and we were inseparable from there.

Seven years after initially-despising James, I married him. That was 15 years ago.

There's a hilarious little cartoon depiction of our story on YouTube. I entered the very first "Why I Love Poker" international competition put on by WPT (World Poker Tour.) I sent in my story about why I love poker, and was one of three chosen finalists in the competition.

My favorite
wedding photo

WPT created a cute little 90-second cartoon based on our stories. You can find the link to the story on my website at: lafayawaypoker.com or by searching Lafaya WPT on YouTube.

I remember thinking when I was first getting to know James, he could and should be one of the professionals I see playing poker on TV (fingers crossed, coming soon.) It baffled me that he wasn't pro. Back then, I however, could not envision myself playing at the professional level. I mean, seriously, I did, and still feel I do not meet the profile.

I'm female, black, a therapist, had three, now six children (no I did not physically give birth to the last three; I adopted my nieces last year), and a traumatic past that many people would never have recovered from. The odds are stacked against me on the daily.

A Glimpse Into a Day in My Life

It's been a hell of a day today. I almost postponed the project of writing this book because I felt overwhelmed with all the day's responsibilities. To give a little context, I made a deal with my publisher to have the book ready to send for print by Saturday, November 30, 2024. That gave me exactly six days to crank out this book.

My son, RJ
Daughter, Myia

My eldest,
Robert

Back in the day, I was dealing with one adult child and two very easy, cave-dwelling teenagers who pressured themselves to get good grades. Hell, I had to talk my daughter down because she was VERY upset about the one "B" she was getting, messing up her 4.0 GPA. Forget worrying about my kids being out too late; I was worried about them hardly ever wanting to go anywhere. And even though they are very attractive kids, they had absolutely NO interest in dating. They definitely did not take after me.

But NOW, I have been blessed with the opportunity to start ALL OVER AGAIN and raise my three little nieces who are VERY different from the kids I gave birth to. At ages four, six, and seven, each of these girls are EXTREMELY social, with flamboyant personalities. They have already taken turns proclaiming who their boyfriends are, (of course, I correct them, letting them know they are not allowed to date until they're 30.)

Anyways, this is a holiday week, so they are not in school; a situation that proves exceptionally inconvenient for trying to write a book.

I woke up around 6 AM and tried to get a little

Ryia Shanna Erial

writing in before it was time for them to wake up. My husband approached me before going to work saying, "Don't get too wrapped up in your writing; you need to eat," and some other blah, blah, wonderful, concerned husband 's words. I gave my typical "yes dear" response and typed away.

My youngest niece, Erial, entered my room first, "Aaaantie, I'm huuuungry." I stopped typing and got up to grab her some breakfast. Maybe about 10 minutes later the oldest, Shanna, came into my room, "Anntie I'm hungry." I told her to take her capable butt into the kitchen and make her own bowl of cereal, then returned to typing again. Riya, the middle one, never came into my room to request breakfast. She made her own cereal. She is the easiest of the three girls and does not require as much attention.

The girls finished breakfast and asked if they could watch TV. I walked into the living room, retrieved the remote from the top of the case we put it on to keep it away from the kids, and turned to the kids Spanish learning channel. They watched an hour of Spanish, an hour of math and then each of them got to choose their own kid appropriate program for 30-minutes each. I went back to writing more content for this book, being interrupted occasionally by tattle-tailing and "look at what I made for you, Auntie."

Before I knew it, it was 11:30 AM, I hadn't eaten nor showered yet, and Erial was at my door saying, "Aaaaantie, I'm hungry again." I was finally able to snap out of my fixation on writing long enough to remember that I hadn't eaten yet and should be hungry. I got up and prepared lunch for myself and the girls letting them know naptime would start at 1 PM. After lunch I let them watch two kids' exercise videos and they were off to nap. My 20-year old daughter, Myia, got home at 1 PM; just in time to stay home with our napping girls. I was proud of myself thinking, 'Okay now I can go start the wash for our weekly seven loads of clothes at the laundromat before my client session at 2 PM.' Clearly, I have no realistic sense of how much time it really takes to get things done, because by the time I was done loading the washers and putting five million quarters into the machines, it was already 2:05 PM. I ran to my car thinking, 'Shit, my session lasts 50 minutes and the washing machines are done in 37 minutes. Oh well, hopefully nobody minds waiting for me to get to my clothes.'

At 2:55, I ran into the wash house to put the seven loads of clothes into the dryer and two million quarters into the machine, all of which took me about 15 minutes. The problem was I had a 3 PM appointment with another client. I called my next client at 3:10 PM, apologizing for my lateness. Luckily, the dryers take 45 minutes to dry, so the wait time wouldn't be so long for anyone waiting to use them.

My next client appointment time was 4:30 PM. I did not want to be late for that appointment, too. So, I called my husband, James, who was now off work, and asked him if he could come help me unload our clothes from the dryer and load them into the car. He came to the rescue, and we made it back to our house just in time for me to have a quick snack before hopping on my 4:30 call. After the call I ran to the store to grab some needed groceries and fried chicken from Save Mart for dinner.

After returning home, I saw a few alerts with correction/clarification requests and approval requests for business cards, etc. from my publisher/ editor, along with a message letting me know that the book needed to be double the length I originally thought it would be. At this point I kind of broke a little. I asked my publisher to give me a call and explained that maybe setting such a close deadline was a mistake. She was able to talk me down and I felt revitalized enough to give this 'making the deadline' thing a go again.

I shared all of this because this is what a working mother of six, who dares to venture out to do anything other than work and raise kids, often has to go through.

In life we run into distractions, roadblocks, things not working out as planned, overwhelming things, etc. daily. Aren't all those things mentioned above a lot like poker? In poker, (especially tournament poker), you run into similar challenges almost every time you sit down to play. Learning how to play the hand you're dealt fits well in poker as well as in life, wouldn't you say?

Taking a look from the outside, you don't see many people like me out there trying to compete on a potentially televised level. But when you get a little glimpse of some insider information, I may be the only person with the weird super combination of things going on that you will see trying to compete at a higher level in poker. To all of us female poker players out there trying to manage a household, take care of children, heal from a traumatic history, and/or the many other obstacles life presents to us AND pursue our dreams of playing professional poker, I'm standing here shouting, "WE GOT THIS!" If I can do it, you can do it. So let's take the poker world by

LAFAYA MITCHELL

storm TOGETHER.

Wisdom From Some Power-Hitting Ladies In Poker

Phenomenal organizations such L.I.P.S and Poker Power have been founded to support the cause of empowering more women poker players.

Poker Power, a rapidly up-and-rising organization, was founded in 2020. Their brand aims to teach poker to women and girls in order to help them advance their careers through power-building strategies learned playing the game of poker. In just four short years, Poker Power has expanded to 40 countries worldwide. On their Instagram page Poker Power recently wrote a post that said, "We know taking calculated risks can be hard especially for career progression. But the more you know about dealing with anxiety when taking risks, [through games like poker], the more confident you'll be." Is that COOL or what? They are truly on a mission to teach that poker skills really do empower us in our lives and careers. Ladies after my own heart!

L.I.P.S. (Ladies International Poker Series) founded

in 2004, just celebrated their 20th anniversary! LIPS is the first, longest running and most popular poker tour in existence for women. LIPS was established to grow the game of poker for women by paving the way for women to learn, practice and excel in the game. Equally important, they have opened up opportunities for women to form bonds, friendships, and a sense of comradery in the mostly male dominated sport of poker. LIPS has formed multiple partnerships with casino operators and other poker industry professionals in order to run poker series events for women worldwide. The newest involves Lady Poker Teams competing against one another in a fun-filled tournament held in April for the past two years.

Badass Women In Poker

Lupe Soto, founder of both of the original female poker organizations Poker Chix & LIPS, as well as the Women in Poker Hall of Fame, took some time out of her insanely busy schedule to bless me with some of her knowledge and wisdom about the game of poker and the game of life.

I'll be sharing Lupe's wisdom, along with great advice from a couple of other hard-hitting female poker professionals Charisse "Pot Hustla" Case, and Cheryl Svenson (3-time WSOP ring winner) who said, "Poker is a women's sport because it's one of the few coed sports where women truly stand equal to men. It's not about physical strength– it's about strategy, intuition, and mental toughness. Women bring unique perspectives to the game, which can often work as an advantage."

What's the top advice you would give to a woman currently playing or wanting to learn to play poker?

Lupe: To find her inner confidence because, if she can be confident while sitting at that table and understand that she's equal to every other person at that table, then she'll be able to enjoy the game. It's never fun to be scared, so if you sit down at the table and you're terrified, 90% of your thought process is going to be about being terrified. All of your thinking energy needs to be dedicated to assessing other people's play; there's no time for fear to get in the way. So, if you can just tap into a situation where you've been confident in the past, whether it was asking for a raise at work or standing up for yourself, capture the way that felt and bring that energy to the poker table, it will go a long way in bringing you energetically closer to playing winning poker. So, I would say confidence is key.

Charisse: Don't let them get in your head. At the table typically it's nine of them [men] and one of us [women.] Play your game and stay focused. DO NOT let them intimidate you because you are 100% equal to those men at the poker table; you're not better and you're not less-than. At the end of the day, they'll either love you or hate you. But, who cares, play your game. You're not there for them. You are there for you and only you.

Cheryl: Do it! Dive in and don't hesitate. It's an incredible game that empowers women to compete equally with men on a level playing field. Build your confidence, learn the strategies, and embrace the thrill of the game.

What's your advice for playing the hand you're dealt in poker and in life?

Lupe: In all aspects of life my advice is, when you know better you do better. I wish more people would take the lessons that they have learned, or are learning, and just apply them. For me that's critical; you have to do that if you're going to have any kind of success in life.

Charisse: Most of us tend to be really anxious to get that big win in poker and in life, but most of the time, it's absolutely about the baby steps. Nothing's going to happen overnight for most people. Poker is a grind, life is a grind. Just stay the course. Every single time I play, I learn something and gain more experience. Focus on learning your experiences and the BIG win will come in more ways than one.

Cheryl: Life and poker can be unpredictable. Don't let "bad beats" get you down. Stay present, adapt when needed and find joy in the opportunity to live and learn another day.

Real life lessons you've learned from playing poker?

Lupe: Poker is a game and you have to keep things in perspective. Even if you're risking important things, like money, it's still a game. You don't want to let a game influence your life to the point where it interrupts your relationships, your work, your faith, or anything else you hold dear.

Charisse: Be disciplined and help keep yourself from making the wrong decision. When you recognize that you're beat you gotta be strong enough to fold and wait for something else better to come along. Just like in real life, you have to know when it's time to let something go and wait for a better time or better opportunity. Sometimes, not being disciplined can come at a really high cost.

Cheryl: Never take anything for granted. Life and poker are full of variance, and every hand is a lesson. Be kind to everyone. You never know when or where you'll cross paths again, and how relationships can impact your journey. Stay alert, stay humble, and keep learning. Poker, like life, is a continual evolution.

What do you love most about the game of poker?

Lupe: Poker can tap into any age group, ethnicity, socio-economic level, sex, disability, etc. It doesn't matter if you're six years old, playing for candy, or 93 years old, being wheeled up to the poker table with an oxygen tank. Almost anybody can play this game.

Charisse: My number one reason for loving poker would be just the rush of it. It's being able to bluff somebody and you know you got away with it. Bluffing somebody with absolutely nothing in your hand and stealing a pot that absolutely didn't belong to you; I enjoy that very much. To me, that's what poker is all about, stealing a pot that doesn't belong to you. That's why my nickname is "Pot Hustla."

Cheryl: Poker is a competitive and exciting game where I get to meet incredible people from all over the world. It's both a social experience and a test of skill, making every game unique and rewarding.

Bio - Cheryl Svenson

Achievements/Successes in Poker Career

• 3 WSOP rings (2 in Ladies Events and 1 in a Bounty Tournament)

• 1 RunGood ring

• 86th place finish in the

Colossus 2015, the largest tournament with a single buy-in, competing against 22,374.

I am a professional poker player and proud business owner of CCMortgage. I've been playing poker for over a decade, achieving major milestones, including winning three WSOP rings and a RunGood ring. I'm also a mother of three amazing children, who are my biggest fans and constant source of inspiration. My journey in poker has been one of growth, learning, and resilience. I'm honored to have my story featured in an upcoming poker book —something I know my dad would be incredibly proud of.

Bio - Lupe Soto

I love poker because it welcomes everyone to the table. Any age group, ethnicity, socio-economic status, disabilities.... And the list keeps going!

In 1996, I cut my teeth on the felt by watching my boyfriend play stud poker on date night. It wasn't long before I was kicking him under the table and telling him how to play his cards. He told me to "go get your own table." I did… and haven't looked back since.

I have a background as a professional therapist and social services administrator. However, once I took a real interest in becoming a poker industry professional and avid poker player, I left that world far behind.

I am the founder of many "firsts" in the poker industry. In 2002, I opened Poker Chix, an online poker forum with an overwhelming positive response from women poker players. This led to the creation of the first women's poker tour, Ladies International Poker Series – LIPS Tour. In 2008 I founded the prestigious Women in Poker Hall of Fame to showcase women who excel in the poker industry as a player or as an industry professional. The "WiPHoF" is embraced by the poker world and stands as one of the greatest honors in the industry.

I also started the first poker tour for seniors, (players over 50 years of age), aptly named "Senior Poker Tour." And, as a tribute to all women poker players, I founded a global association: Women's Poker Association, a 501c3 Non-Profit created to elevate and empower all women in poker.

If you were to ask me to describe myself, I would say

> "I am round, brown, and low to the ground… With a passion for people and poker."

Bio - Charisse "Pot Hustla" Case

I began playing poker in 2014. Some friends of mine were hosting Wednesday night poker, and I decided to stop by one night. By the end of the night, I knew right then…I was hooked. It's been nonstop poker since. After about a year of playing the home game, I finally built up enough courage to walk into Capital Casino in downtown Sacramento. I jumped in a $1/3 no-limit table and pretty much got my ass handed to me. Well, that got old fast, so I began reading, watching videos, and really paying attention to plays on televised poker. Boy did that help! Fast forward to July 2018, I decided to take the leap and quit working to play poker full-time. I was a document production coordinator for an environmental consulting firm for many years. I loved my job, but I became so passionate about poker that I made it my new career. I enjoy both cash games and tournaments.

As for tournaments, I haven't hit a BIG one yet, but I'm well on my way. I recently place 2nd in the World Series of Poker Circuit ring event in Lake Tahoe, Nevada; 3rd in the World Poker Tour Leaning

Tower of Chips event at Thunder Valley; 1st in the Ante Up Poker Tour No Limit Holdem event at Atlantis, Reno; Final tabled a Heartland Poker Tour event in Blackhawk, Colorado; and have final tabled numerous other events.

I'm a mother of two beautiful adult children and I have an incredible man who supports me very much. My family, my dog, our horses, and our beautiful home surrounded by pine trees are everything to me. Good luck to all and hope to see you on the felt.

Only The Strong Survive

Poker is definitely not meant for the weak at heart. You have to literally be prepared to take an ass whoopin' on the regular and keep coming back until it's your turn to kick a little ass. If you care about, or have a problem with things being unfair, you are playing the wrong sport. Bad beats are the norm in this game. The best players in the world only win approximately 15% of the time. There are NO guarantees; if you play the game long enough, that statistical 93% chance to win at the flop or turn, can and will turn into a 0% chance to win on many rivers.

Hilariously, the variance of the game is only a small portion of the hell that can come along with daring to venture to be a decent poker player. After all of the studying and attempts to stay in-the-know about the most up-to-date GTO (Game Theory Optimal) strategies, you WILL NOT become or stay successful in poker if you do not address the mental aspect of the game.

The robots of the game (those mostly devoid of emotions) have an edge over us more passionate personality types. Those who also have none, to very little other responsibilities in life, (other than poker), have a HUGE advantage over those of us who live in more of a "real world" kind of situation.

For women, in particular, our real-world responsibilities typically include work, home management, child management, other family member management, nurturer, cook, spouse pleaser…. Our HUGE to-do lists usually must be addressed, and addressed well before we even think about going to play poker.

Here's another real-life example. My morning journal, November 23, 2024:

Rough Morning: I am having a fit of "imposter syndrome." I mean, what in the world does a person like me have to say that other people will even care about? I have been trying for years to figure out how to get "The Lafaya Way" out there and none of that shit has worked to a significant degree, yet. Is writing another book supposed to help? What makes me have the nerve to think that I am supposed to be doing anything other than taking care of my six kids (aged 4-32 years; five still live at home with me, not including my son's best friend who also lives with us and calls me mom.)

I am literally in my living room, computer on my lap, trying to meet the deadline for writing this damn book. My four-year-old niece/daughter (adopted her in November) is watching "Team Umi Zumi" in the background. It's Saturday and, of course, she woke up bright and early. It's a bad day for this waking up early shit because I have a Live show to promote the new book I recently helped co-author, "SPEECHLESS: Giving the #voiceless a Voice" in 1.5 hours, a list of things to get to my publisher for this book ASAP, and a smidge of a hangover from the strong drinks I ordered to meet the 2-drink minimum required when you attend comedy shows at Punchline (Chad Daniels is freaking HILARIOUS!) Also, just now, believe it or not, my niece-daughter just informed me that she is now hungry, so apparently, I'll need to get up and make her something to eat because I do not currently have a freaking nanny…

Okay, I'm back. LOL… BUT *now* my 20-year-old daughter, who is a dancer, just walked in the room asking me where her jeans with the holes in the knees are because they're a part of her outfit for a K-Pop themed performance she is leaving to do in San Jose today. Oh, and she also needs gas money to get to her event. WTF! Go find your own jeans and your own gas money while you're at it, grown-up child!

AND, oh shit, I now only have 30 minutes left until I need to be in the Streamyard studio for my Live. I still need a shower, nice shirt to wear, and to set up the area I'll be Zooming from. Forget about doing my hair; I guess today will be a headband and no make-up day. This will be a true Beyonce moment: I did wake up like this!

Does any of what I just described sound familiar to you? The list above is just the tip of the iceberg for most women. Lots of us have to manage our career, husband, bills, laundry, cleaning, cooking, grocery shopping, EVERYTHING involved with raising kids (appts, school issues, hair, what to wear, etc.) .... Okay, you probably get my point by now.

I basically live in constant "Red Alert Brain" (crisis) mode on the daily. Playing poker is not a sport that helps ease the "Red Alert Brain" state. As a matter of fact, the volatility of poker can catapult us directly into red alert status. Even some of the calmest personality types out there occasionally fall victim to poker tilt. I once watched this super Zen dude go from peace and love to pissed off in a matter of three hands played.

It takes extreme resilience, determination, and an unphased supply of hope, with a sprinkle of crazy, to persist in playing poker at a competitive level. Poker wears us down mentally so we need access to every tool we can get to beat the game.

As you will see, so much about the game of poker is similar to dealing with life's challenges. I even considered calling this book "Life lessons learned from poker" because you can easily apply the following to everyday life.

The Lafaya Way

The Lafaya Way 4 Core Steps:

Think of The Lafaya Way 4 Core Steps like the ingredients to a cake. If you're missing an ingredient you end up with a flat, ugly, and/or flat-out nasty cake. On the other hand, when you put all of the ingredients together, you end up with something DELICIOUS.

The acronym I use to help recall the 4 Core Steps more quickly is:

F.U.R.R.

F- Find Your Calm
U- Understand the Real Truth
R- Respond in Alignment w/Your Truest Intentions
R- The 3 Rs: Recognize Small Step Improvements, Reinforce Improvements Highly, Re-cycle through the 4 Steps.

Step 1: Find Your Calm

Ok. I'm not gonna lie, this first step is one I step into carefully. Being a more passionately reactive (hot-headed) person, I can appreciate the frustration with being told to calm down during an emotionally-explosion moment.

This is one of the BIG reasons behind my choosing the wording *Find* your calm. What I've found is that it's not impossible to calm down; it's just REALLY hard depending on how far into crisis mode you are. We can develop a plan and be proactive about creating "lifelines"— something to grab hold of so that we don't fall into the gaping blackhole our emotions can become.

Emotional black holes are spotted all over the place for hypersensitive people such as myself. One of the common attacks on a sensitive person's system is having to be around, or deal with, negative energy coming from others. Hypersensitive people tend to be plagued by a phenomenon that I call "Emotion-Soaking." Emotion-Soaking is the unintentional sponging of the "feeling" energies of those around you. (Picture a flat sponge reflecting no negative emotion transfer and an enlarged sponge that has soaked in someone's negative energy transfer.)

There is often a mega ton of negative energy at the poker table. Every poker table typically has at least one douche-hole sitting at it. Finding your calm is important to prevent and/or cool the effects of being triggered by ass-holes, bad beats, unlucky dealers, bad floor decisions, annoying texts received while at the table, etc.

> *Our brain's default reaction to being triggered at the poker table is T.I.L.T.*

We have the right to choose to override that system and go into the more calming problem-solving mode.

Two main keys to Finding Your Calm include:

1.   Don't Personalize. As mentioned earlier on in this book, taking on someone else's issues, struggles, mistakes (their shit) and then making it about you, instead of keeping their problems about them, can be detrimental to your ability to be calm. It is impossible to feel offended, disrespected, and/or mistreated and calm at the same time. However, shifting to logical thoughts such as, 'Acting/playing the way they are will lead to bad results for them over the long run,' will help keep you on the pathway to Peace Road and away from the Highway to Tilt City.

Is thinking in this way VERY difficult to do, especially in a heated moment? Hell YES! However, it is not impossible and gets easier with practice. I mean, did LeBron James pick up the basketball the first time and have amazing handles? No. He practiced his butt off until he was the best; then when he was the best, he still kept practicing, keeping his edge.

2. Monitor and Balance your Physical Cues to Upset. Some physical cues to upset include: pounding/ racing heart, shallow breathing, tensing muscles, heating up (feeling extra hot.) These physical cues

send a message to the brain that the body is in danger and in need of protection which then kicks flight/fight into gear. It's an ancient protective mechanism built into the brain for survival (i.e.: see dinosaurs, hide, run, fight or die!)

With no impending doom, it is important to slow down the red alert effects that happen in the brain and body by first thinking, 'Ok, no sabertooth tiger chasing me, so this racing heart, shallow breathing, etc., is just telling me something that happened that I didn't like very much.'

Tips for countering cues to upset:

First things first: take a deep breath (inhale five count, exhale six count, or, pick a deep breathing technique you like.) Deep breathing is a 3-fer: it counters shallow breathing, gets more oxygen to the brain to improve your ability to think, and helps to slow down that speedy heart rate.

Another physical cue balancing action is to relax your muscles: un-ball those fists, relax those shoulder muscles and wherever else it is you are holding tension. If you're hot, take a bathroom break, dampen a towel with cold water and rub it against your skin. If you are feeling particularly antsy, impatient or agitated at the table (hint: you start playing hands you wouldn't typically play or shouldn't be playing, trying to force the game), take a walk to cool off. For some players, using headphones or fidget spinners can assist with battling the antsies.

Basically, countering the cues to upset is exactly as it sounds: DO something non-harmful to yourself or others to battle the flood of physical cues that show up when you're being triggered into TILT mode.

Step 2: Understand the "REAL" Truth

As mentioned above, the 4 Core Steps work together like the ingredients in a cake. Understanding the Real Truth is also a great way to assist with Finding Your Calm. Getting to the REAL truth is often not as simple as it sounds, though. There are many 'think they're truths' we tell ourselves that are more based in perception, (which varies for everyone), than they are in the real truth.

It can be VERY tough to get to the "real" truth.

Two Keys:

1. Use helpful check-ins such as H.A.L.T. (from 12-steps program)

Hungry
Angry
Lonely
Tired

Any of the states above can cause amplified

emotions, thus, we become more easily triggered. When we're able to identify the TRUE reasons behind our STRONG feelings, it keeps us from completely blaming the situations and circumstances outside of ourselves for the intensity of our feelings. This, in turn, gives us more control over managing how we feel. If we perceive someone or something outside of ourselves as at-fault for how we feel, it takes away our ability to better manage how we feel. However, when we can attach something that is within our control (i.e. hunger), this helps assist us in more quickly finding our calm. The check-ins cause us to better identify where our strong emotions are coming from and also help us to problem-solve on how to improve future situations for ourselves (i.e. "Next time I'll make sure I get a good night's sleep before coming to play poker.")

2.   Ask yourself questions that cause you to take a deeper look into yours and others' reactions.

> A. Is insecurity at play? Sometimes we/they may feel a little embarrassed about a mistake made which makes us more reactive in the moment. Embarrassment can really turn up the volume on emotions.
>
> B. Are there struggles/issues at home? One of my favorite go-to thoughts to move me out of disliking and feeling negative feelings towards another player, (which impacts my game), is 'They must be

cranky because they're not getting any at home.'

C. Is there something from my/their past that may cause me/them to be more easily triggered? For example, I have a history of being extremely sensitive to feeling treated like I'm dumb or less-than. Being both black and female, I have run into many situations where people would treat me as if I need to have things over-explained, (women often call this man-splaining when a man does it), apparently because I couldn't be smart enough to understand. I used to be highly offended by this, but now I let it go, understanding that other people's thoughts and opinions are just THEIR thoughts and opinions; they have nothing to do with me.

D. Are they emotional "stimmers"? For particularly annoying people that seem to get extremely reinforced by causing negative reactions in others, "emotional stimming" might be at play. Emotional Stimming is seeking after strong sensory input by way of evoking strong internal emotional reactions from others. For those that engage in it, this type of stimming is very self-sabotaging. Try to keep in mind that all humans NEED to feel connected, loved, and understood. If anyone appears as if they don't need or care about these things, an injury has occurred at some point that surely causes them a great deal of pain.

Understanding the "real" truth requires that you ask yourself questions which allow you to acquire deeper insight into your own as well as other's experiences. The better you are at keeping things in perspective, the less inclined you will be to be swallowed up by big black holes of emotion.

Step 3: Respond in Alignment with Your Truest Intentions

I remember how I used to "play myself" all the time. I'd pridefully fight against my own desires, oblivious to the fact that I was actually more responsible for not getting my needs met than the person I was blaming for not meeting my needs.

I would vehemently lash out at others, blind to the fact that none of this behavior helped me to meet my needs. As a matter of fact, the more negative energy I put out, the more negative juju I got back. I literally can not remember a time when I was being extremely negative and actually won a tournament. My wins almost always come on the days that I am feeling positive, thus drawing positive energy my way. You get more of what you put your energy into.

Responding in alignment with your truest desires has to be done with intention. You must have a recognized target in order to hit said target. You can't just put "somewhere" in your GPS and expect that it'll take you to the location you would like to get to. In life, if you are not clear on, or keep your gaze on, your core goals, you often can't stay true to being intentional about getting what you want.

I once asked one of the greatest poker players of all time, Andrew Lichtenberger, aka: "LuckyChewy," how he was able to handle dealing with assholes so well. Chewy was one of the instructors working with me and about 30 other students in a live LearnWPT training. I was SUPER impressed by how truly unphased he was by this jerky guy who would challenge every instruction he was given. I asked him how he was able to stay so calm. He shared that peace is a state that he is constantly intentional about seeking. He meditates daily and recommended I do the same if I wanted a better chance at keeping my peace. I believe LuckyChewy to be a guy who has truly mastered the art of responding in alignment with his truest intentions, and I am confident this plays a big part in his success as a poker player.

Keys to Responding in Alignment with Your Truest Intentions:

1. Ask yourself, 'What are my core goals?'

—Stop for a moment and list Core Goals that you may have at the poker table—

2. Actively DO something daily to move you closer to achieving your identified core goals.

3. Empowerment Self-Talk:

My goal is to___   (core goal which applies to current situation)

My goal is not to___ (behaviors that may be working against you)

When I___   (unhelpful behavior)

It causes___   (unwanted result)

And I know that is not my intention.

So, I will___instead (more productive replacement behavior)

Empowerment Self Talk example:

My goal is to win this tournament, which requires focus
My goal is not to engage in unfruitful conversation with this numbnut at the table
When I try to talk to prove a dumbass wrong at the table
It messes with my focus, ultimately leading to my

losing chips
And I know that is not my intention.
So, I'll put on my headphones and drown out his stupid voice, instead.

Keeping in mind our core goals, actively engaging in activities to help achieve our identified goals, and using the self-empowerment talk formula, can go a long way to help us function in better alignment with our truest intentions.

Step 4: 3-Rs = Recognize, Reinforce, Repeat

Step 4 is my Growth-Mindset step. It brings light and hope to tough situations by focusing on small step improvements as opposed to focusing on the problems that still exist. This step is good at battling perfectionism and all-or-nothing thinking.

3-R Breakdown

Recognize — Recognizing the "small step" wins increases your faith in the possibility of positive change. Make a consistent effort to acknowledge when there's been progress. The alternative is to expect overall/perfection/huge leap changes and constantly feeling disappointed that you are not reaching your goal.

Reinforce — Highly reinforce the positive changes that you see. Reinforcement serves to:

- Build self-esteem (a Yes, I can do this spirit)
- Put more energy into the things we want more of
- Keep us properly balanced (opens us up to recognizing the positive more readily)

> Instinctually, humans tend to be highly reactive to those things that are perceived as "danger." It is our survival instinct (see dinosaur, must avoid the danger.) Translate the 'danger' experience to poker, where unwanted results "make" you "feel" not so good, so you must "do" something about it. We are not instinctually reactive to those things that are the "safe" things (i.e., expected/desired results.) Often when we get "desired" results it does not elicit a strong (survival instinct-type) response from us, so it can often but unintentionally go ignored.

For example: 'Step 4ing it' in poker means recognizing that my being pissed off about taking a bad beat looks VERY DIFFERENT now than it did not that long ago. I've gone from full on meltdowns, which included cussing out the other players, the dealer, and anybody else who had the nerve to make a comment; to holding it in at the table and then scream-crying while punching the roof of my car all the way home; to speeding dangerously fast on the freeway, verbally unleashing my anger out on 'bad drivers,' to NOW yelling "FUCK" a couple of times in the car, turning my favorite song way up and singing out all the bad energy. Those incremental small step improvements are worth acknowledging and patting myself on the back. Acknowledging small improvements keeps me from judging myself for getting upset when I should 'know better than being upset about a game,' and gives me hope that I'll be able to one day display the classy demeanor of respected world champions.

Repeat/Re-cycle/Recalibrate: Stay aware of the importance of constantly flowing through (working) the 4 Core Steps. The 4-Steps are on-going.

Working the 4-Steps is an excellent way to Level UP your Mental Game!

The next few chapters will discuss issues commonly encountered by poker players. Problem solving, using the 4-Steps, is woven throughout.

Poker Couples: The Good, The Bad, And The Ugly

"I know this fool did NOT call my pre-flop raise with Q-8! He ain't got no respect at all. That's OK, cause I won't be folding many hands to his raises in the future. I don't care if I only like the hand a little bit, I'm calling his bitch-ass raise Ugh!"

I'm sure you guessed it. These are some of the thoughts I had about my husband's play at a recent tournament in which I was stuck, yet again, playing at a poker table against him. Man, he makes me sick sometimes; and I'm sure he has his days of not liking me much, too. LOL!

I had raised 3x the blinds first to act, another player called my raise and James called from the cutoff. Long story short, the hand ended in such a way that James won a huge pot from the donk who called in the middle of us. I was a little agitated that the pot would have been mine if James had stayed out of the hand in the first place. I thought Q-8 was a pretty loose call against a first to act raiser; I likely would not make the same call against his raise, even if another player was in the mix.

Now, the honest truth is, James and I are different players with different play styles; we already agreed a long time ago to play our games and not alter our play because we're playing against each other. An even larger truth is, "AIN'T NO FRIENDS IN POKER!" It is each player's goal to be the last person standing. This means that ALL chips in the tournament are up for grabs, including those being held by spouses, best friends, children we have given birth to, etc.

It took me a LONG time to finally calm down about the 'no friends in poker' rule. In times past I would get REALLY upset with some of my friends about ways they played against me at the poker table. Before I started playing any semblance of winning poker, I thought it wasn't okay to play against my friends the same way I would any stranger out there. The reality is, losing focus on the prize (winning ALL the chips) is a HUGE mistake in poker.

Over the years, James and I have had numerous conversations about times we altered our play a bit because the other was in the hand… and how it cost us chips. Many times, the other players in the hands with us would end up with the chips because we were trying to "respect" each other's bets or raises. After a bunch of discussions about hands we finally came to the conclusion we both have to allow the other to play their game in order to be playing our best poker. He knew this all along; my sensitive self on the other hand, needed a few years to stop reacting badly when I thought he'd slighted me at the poker table.

So many people have expressed their admiration about our relationship. They'll say things like, "You're so lucky that your wife/husband likes poker, too." The truth is relationships are relationships: it takes intentional work to be happy in any relationship. It can help or hurt to have things like poker in common, depending on how you deal with it.

Some of the keys to maintaining happiness as a poker couple are:
- True acceptance of each other's quirks, different styles of play, different personalities and all
- Value happiness over the need to be right; getting along is our priority
- Do not expect perfection; there will be good days and there will be bad days
- Don't go to bed angry
- Communication focused on the solution, not the problem
- Focus on the good more than the bad; cover every bad thought with two good ones
- Do not let anything get in the way of couples fun time, intimate time, date nights, and kid free vacations

James and I have been together for about 15

years. We have had good days, bad days, and days where we didn't think we would make it as a couple. The strains on our relationship have been numerous (cultural, parenting styles, poker disagreements, mental health, financial

decisions, stepkids, adopting my three little nieces, extended family issues, etc.)

It has been no easy task to get to where we are today. It sure is worth it, though.

This journey as a poker couple has yielded some pretty STELLAR experiences.

How we won the "7 Days to Vegas" prize package:

I was at work and got a fairly frantic call from James. He says, "Babe, what time are you off work today? I'm playing this "7 Days to Vegas" tournament and doing pretty well, but have to leave for work in about an hour." I said, "I still have one client session left, but I'll rush straight home after we're done." My therapy sessions generally last 45-50 mins. He said, "OK, HURRY." I finished up with my client and sped home. As I walked in the door, he was handing me the computer and rushing to his car. As luck would have it, the tournament had just gone on a five minute break, giving me a chance to settle myself in and finish up the tournament for him.

The tournament started with over 2000 entries and there were only about 200 players remaining. I was SOOO NERVOUS. I did not want to mess up by losing after he had gotten so far. I played my paranoid style of play (the opposite of how James plays) and avoided several disastrous set-up hands. My paranoia about on-line gaming caused me to fold quite a few "good" hands instead of staying in to see the flop. In turn, I played quite a few "bad" hands very well and got opponents to fold in key situations. My belief is that if James were there playing the end portion that was left for me, we very likely would not have won the package. Long story, short, we won first place in the tournament, which awarded us the first free VIP package available for the "7 Days to Vegas" experience. I called James to give him the good news and could hear all of his fellow staff cheering for us in the background. He had been telling them all about our tournament, a two person relay race in which he had to pass the baton to me. GOOO Team Mitchell!

The "7 Days to Vegas" VIP package included: an all expenses paid trip to Las Vegas to watch the movie premiere, walk the red carpet, play a freeroll tournament against all of the other various VIP package winners and a few famous poker players with bounties on their heads, enjoy a fancy club-style environment meal, rub elbows with a few of poker's finest elite players plus other goodies. We had an absolute BALL!

As a couple, we have had to deal with the same struggles as any other couple. However, being a poker couple has added a few more obstacles to happy coupling. Through it all we have been able to persevere and even thrive because we practice what I preach in this book.

Ok, wait, this just happened and I had to share it with you: My husband just took a quick look at the computer, saw the 1st paragraph and said, "Fool, huh?" I said, "Yea, fool is light; I opened a different chapter calling somebody a mother fucker. Fool is light." He explained how we had already been there, done that, talked it to death about not playing each other 'light' at the poker table. I explained to him I know that, but was using how I initially felt in that particular moment to lead into my discussion about there not being room for friends or friendly play at the poker table. James then defended, "We hardly ever get into many hands together, anyway." I responded, "Yea, I'll be in plenty of your hands in the future, with your Q-8 playing self." He retorted, "Well then come on in, I like free chips, suckafish." LOL! [We do love talking a little shit when it comes to poker.]

Poker, Gambling And Addiction

OOweee. The subject of gambling and addiction is a tough one for me. I REALLY wanted to go play poker this morning, but I have five million other things to do. All of the content for this very book I am writing right now is due by tomorrow. I don't really have time for a tournament. The pull to play is so strong it causes such a strong emotional response that it literally feels like physical pain in my body when I can't go. This helps me to understand, at least where I am concerned, the addictive component to playing poker. I know that I am genetically predisposed to addiction because my parents were some serious addicts.

Even though I'm aware that poker has its addictive component, for some reason, it still bothers me to no end when outsiders refer to tournament poker as gambling. I'm just not sold on the idea that playing tournament poker, in-and-of-itself, is gambling in the way outsiders mean it. People who don't play tournament poker tend to compare it to slot play and Bingo; both of those are based purely on luck, with no skill required. You can't bluff a slot machine or induce a Bingo ball to make a wrong decision. There are strategies, (GTO is currently the most popular strategy), to apply in competitive poker play. Learning and applying the best strategies exponentially improves your chances of playing winning poker.

The side to poker that typically gets players into trouble is its addictive draw. Poker requires gambling at different levels given the situation at times. Each hand played is a gamble because there is no 100% chance of winning before the hand begins; winning depends on whether or not the combination of your hole cards and the cards on the board fall in your favor. The best odds poker can give us, preflop, is about an 88% chance to win, with the best starting hand in the game going up against the worst possible starting hand in the game.

There are a couple of additional areas worth mentioning and which contribute to addiction in poker. Getting away with HUGE bluffs can give us poker players quite a rush. The bigger the bluff, the bigger the rush. The high from a great bluff can last for long periods of time. The other area I'll mention here is similar to what happens with people who play slot machines. I'll call it the "I almost had it" syndrome. If we've been playing poker long enough we have heard plenty of players, including ourselves say things like, "I was so close" or "all I needed was one more ___ to win." Poker players have even adopted terms like Chinese straight= four cards to a straight, instead of the five cards to a straight needed to actually count as an official straight. The "I was so close" syndrome often tricks us into the realm of magical thinking (having a feeling of "almost" winning, which keeps us close to winning, without the actual win.)

Playing poker basically involves gambling every single hand you play, (whether you're bluffing or not), so the causes of addiction often come into play. Gambling activates the brain's reward system, which releases dopamine, a neurotransmitter that produces feelings of pleasure and excitement whether you win or you lose.

When there are obstacles to my going to play poker when I want to, my bratty inner child often screams out things like, "Aw man, I can't never do nothin'!" I feel all the feelings attached to disappointment. The interesting part is the feelings are very real; my inner kid really is disappointed by the fact that we aren't going to get the nice dopamine boost that comes along with gambling. Dopamine boost means excitement. Taking it away can cause feelings equivalent to a child being told to get dressed to go to Disneyland and then being told, 'Nevermind, maybe later.'

Because of its natural pull on us, it can be excessively difficult to, as they say, "gamble responsibly." A few suggestions for trying to do so include:

> ❖ Avoid being in denial about the addictive component to any gambling. Since there is no 100% chance of winning the game, and there are stakes involved, you are gambling.
> ❖ Don't be ashamed of the fact that we gamble. It causes us to hide our behaviors which keep us from sharing our behaviors with others.
> ❖ Appoint a very honest person you can trust to always tell you the truth no matter what; someone willing to check-in with you about your behaviors around gambling, if only for the sake of accountability.
> ❖ Give yourself short vacations from gambling; try enjoying time with friends or family who don't gamble during these "vacations."

The above check-list of things can help you keep perspective, which in turn reduces the likelihood you will engage in problem gambling.

Signs of problem gambling include:

Cognitive distortions
People with gambling problems may develop cognitive distortions, such as believing they'll eventually win if they keep gambling.

Loss aversion
People are more sensitive to losses than gains of equal value. This can lead gamblers to try to win

back losses, which can create a vicious cycle.

Illusion of control
Gamblers may believe they have special skills or knowledge that give them an advantage.

Signs of compulsive gambling or gambling disorder include:
- Continually chase bets that lead to losses
- Use up savings and create debt
- Hiding behavior
- Turning to theft or fraud to support the addiction
- Experiencing feelings of anxiety, stress, or agitation around one's gambling habit, especially when something prohibits getting to their "fix."
- Betting more than one can afford to lose

Serious gambling issues have led to loss of homes, cars, relationships, jobs, time in prison, and even death by way of physical health or owing the wrong people money. It is wise to seek professional help if gambling gets out of control.

Self-Care Is Important
To Winning In Poker

My dumb ass did it again just the other day! I failed to honor my pre-tournament self-care check-list. My check-list is a list of five things. Did you eat? Do you have easily accessible childcare for the girls? Have you exercised in the past three days? Do you have any pressing matters to deal with that take priority/Is your schedule clear? Do you anticipate any potential distractions?

What my morning looked like before I attended the above tournament:

I scrambled around my house multi-tasking as usual. The kids needed breakfast, hair dues, and proper outfits. The house was a mess. I had been working on content for my book from 6a-10a; the tournament start time was 10a with a 20 minute drive to get there.There was no one home to watch the girls; my daughter had stayed the night at her friends' house (I literally had to call and have her come home before I could leave to be late for the tournament.) AND, most importantly, not only had I not been to the gym in four days, I also skipped breakfast. With all of these things stacked against me, I decided, yep I'm going to accept these less than optimal circumstances to go play a tournament that requires intense focus and concentration anyway.

Now clearly the therapist in me was thinking, "Lafaya, this is a bad idea; you know you don't do well when you're hangry." However, the bratty little kid in me said, "You'll be fine, you can just order something to eat while you're at the poker table."

I arrived at the tournament an hour late and ended up out the door in record time. I sat at the table highly agitated, distracted, and low energy all at the same time. I probably couldn't have won a game of Go Fish in that state, let alone poker.

As I walked my losing ass out the door, I couldn't help but think about this book; how I definitely needed to add a chapter about self-care in a book focused on the mental game of poker.

Lack of self-care blocks the ability to focus, make good decisions, and regulate emotions. This makes you more susceptible to making poor strategic choices, potentially resulting in losing all of your chips and/or over the long-term burnout.

Self-care should be done proactively; in preparation for the mentally demanding nature of tournament poker. Some self-care suggestions include:

1. The top two on most lists: Good diet and regular exercise

2. Daily meditation or listening to affirmations
3. Prioritize good sleep habits; feeling rested also improves your mood in general, and your coping ability increases dramatically
4. Warm baths (include bath bombs and such for aromatherapy effects)
5. Get a nice massage
6. Identify 3-5 things you are thankful for every morning
7. Make it a point to take a nap or relax midday every once in awhile
8. Read a good book (non-poker related) every once in awhile
9. Plan to take at least one vacation per year (a real getaway from work and poker)
10. Take a break from watching the news and/or exposing yourself to other programs/people that elicit a lot of negative feelings. The goal is to smile/laugh which has the effect of boosting mood and reducing stress levels. Try watching comedy shows, instead.

Here are a few things you can do to assist yourself during tough moments in poker tournaments as well:

1. Take a walk when needed
2. Listen to your favorite upbeat music

3. Take a prolonged, deep inhale/exhale after a tough beat to clear the previous hand from memory

It Ain't the Dealer's / Donkey's Fault??

"This motha fucka has to be working cards." I cannot lie and say that this conspiracy theory thought has not crept into my head on more than 100 occasions. LOL. Embarrassingly, I have a long history of blaming the dealer for my losses. Holding the dealer responsible for losses is definitely something that negatively affects our game play.

Dealer-blaming often causes us to:

- Lose our focus on the game at hand. We tend to stop player watching and start dealer watching instead, leaving a clear pathway for more savvy players to take advantage of our distraction.
- Hold angry/negative/victim energy — Negative energy does not typically draw positive juju; we get more of what we put our energy into. Also, the sharks at the table can sense blood and nothing provokes attacks more than a wounded victim in the water.

- Miss out on the opportunity to properly evaluate and improve our own game — It is impossible to blame someone else and engage in personal growth at the same time. Putting our energy into recognizing whether we could have played the hand any better is a much more fruitful use of our energy. If, after evaluating the hand and running the hand by a better/equal player than us, we recognize we could not have played the hand any better, then acknowledging that variance is a huge part of the game [and, given the best players in the world only win 15-20% of the time] is a much more useful thought than, 'This dealer HATES me' or 'This game SUCKS!'

I originally started working on reducing my dealer blaming after getting a chance to be the dealer myself in a few home games. I dealt HORRIBLY to myself. After dealing quite a few truly bad beats to myself and thinking afterwards, "Who is dealing this shit? Oh yea, that would be me," I had to acknowledge that maybe there was no malicious intent nor conspiracy going on with certain dealers (yes, I had three or four dealers pegged as cheaters at the time.)

The next encouragement not to blame the dealers came when I recorded a few episodes for my creation, "The Lafaya Way Poker Show." One of the cast members, a dealer friend, "Mr. Big Deal," dealt the hands to our "Poker Roundtable" crew and guests. I did short interviews with each of our cast members discussing poker issues. My dealer friend was interviewed on dealer issues, of course. He spoke to the frustration of having to constantly deal with being accused of being a dirty or "bad" dealer. Mr. Big Deal spoke frankly about the fact that many players accusing him of being a bad dealer usually engaged in making poor decisions during play and were just looking for someone else to blame. He went on to explain that he just deals the cards; he can't help what cards come out.

My own experience of dealing to myself BADLY, and the interview with Mr. Big Deal, were big time eye openers for me. I can't say that I don't have a couple of dealers that I still HATE to see coming my way because, for one reason or another, they are like poker cancer to me. I can, however, say that I am no longer highly suspicious of them; no longer think all kinds of terrible things about them, such as hoping that a small truck might fall on their heads. It also helps to use the "bad dealer's" time dealing (dealers are usually rotated to different tables after a set period of time, typically every 40-60 mins) to get more into observing and taking mental notes on other players' styles so that I can build strategic plans for future play.

It is equally as important not to blame the "Donkey" for our losses. Negatively focusing on other players' supposed bad plays does not help us win. It is imperative we keep our eyes on the prize. Our ultimate goal is to be the last person standing.

There have definitely been times when I have gotten really upset with another person's donk play. So I try to get revenge, hoping to give that player a dose of their own medicine (this makes me now the donk, correct?) To do so usually requires abandoning my own style of play, sound strategy, and common sense; basically, I am on TILT. When I fall into this emotional trap, my loss is usually imminent. Either I get beat by the so-called donk himself or by another player who has entered the hand. Astute players will often recognize when other players are battling against one another and jump in to take advantage of their tunnel vision pursuit. Usually, over the long term, the sounder-minded players prevail. Thus, donk-hunting is definitely the opposite of Step 3ing it, (Step 3: Respond vs React) and is not an effective strategy for winning in poker.

The real truth is poker wouldn't be poker without our dear donkeys out there to, more times than not, donate their chips to us who are willing to wait them out.

Poker Is A SICK SICK Game

Son of a fuckin bitch! I just got knocked out of the tournament by deuce-four of spades.

SOOOO fuckin annoying. We were playing the hand before the bubble vote. It was my big blind. Blinds were 4k-8k and the button shoves his 12k into the pot. Small blind doesn't notice the raise and adds 4k to complete what he thought was a call to 8k. The dealer told him he needed to put out 4k more to call and the dude hesitated a bit and then called. I looked at my big blind and had Q-7 clubs. My first instinct said shove, but I overrode that with, 'Let's see if one of us can knock this guy out.' The flop comes Qs-8s-5h. I thought I had Q-8 in my hand (2 pair) and shoved 25k without double-checking. Small blind calls my shove and flips over 2s-4s (a fucked up flush draw) and I flipped over Q-7 to my own surprise. Of course, the turn card is Ks to complete his baby flush, and the river is 8h to make me even more pissed. If I actually had the hand I thought I had the river would have made my full house to beat his punk-ass flush.

Basically, this one hand cost me big time; it was

beyond a bad beat. A guy who never should have been in the hand in the first place knocked me out, making me the last person to be eliminated before everyone else split their share of the winnings.

I muttered "this is bullshit" and fast-walked my losing ass out of the door, promptly called my husband and vented about how that raggedy ass donk called with four high got rewarded. During my long drive home I was able to process the hand to see if there was anything I could have/should have done better in the hand.

The two top conclusions I came to were:

1. I should have followed my first instinct and shoved pre-flop when the dude showed weakness and hesitation to call the additional 4k. This would have gotten a player with more chips than me out of the hand, and set me up to go heads up against a player who could not knock me out of the tournament. (Instead, I double-bubbled with the other loser.)

2. I should not have taken a "team" approach to knock another player out because the truth is the other player I "teamed up" with was sure happy to knock my punk ass out right along with the other guy. Poker is a lone wolf game. Like Tech N9ne says in his song, "Fuck everybody, but me."

It's okay to be pissed off when you take what feels like an unnecessary loss; own that upset. My very

WISE friend, Lonnee Rey, once said to me, "You can't let go of what you don't own."

Applying The Lafaya Way steps is key to growing from your losses. A great starter question to ask is similar to the question I asked above, "What can I learn from this loss?" Here's a breakdown of how asking this one question leads you directly into the 4 Steps:

Finding Your Calm — Moving into problem-solving mode reduces emotional reactivity, feelings of victimization and personalization.

Understanding the Real Truth — Seeking to learn from the loss helps to identify possible areas of needed improvement and/or basic truths about the game (i.e. high variance, luck is a HUGE component, if you're playing at the level you should be playing life is not ruined by this one hand; live to play another day, etc.)

Responding in Alignment w/Your Truest Intentions — Even though our ultimate goal is to win, a close 2nd is to learn from our losses to give us a better chance to win in the future. We'll be engaging with the secondary goal more often than the first because, like I said earlier, the best players in the world only win approximately 15% of the time. Our goal is to not be pissed off 85% or more of the time playing this game, go on T.I.L.T constantly, nor hate the game we love.

3-Rs (Recognize, Reinforce, Repeat) — When you bypass or reduce emotional upset and/or meltdown behavior by asking a clarifying question, recognize the growth and maturity it took to get there, be proud of yourself for your improvement no matter how small and remember working the four steps is a process.

You're not looking for perfection. You're looking to focus more on the positive small step changes, which boosts self-esteem, belief in self, and hope for an incrementally better, more emotional pain-free existence.

The best part is, if you apply these steps in any area of your life, it will yield incrementally better results for you.

As in poker, so in life.

Surviving Red Alert Brain

"I cannot believe this!" I felt a combination of shock and utter horror as I walked away from the table. Even the other players at the table looked like they felt sorry for my losing ass. I was playing in the WPT Ladies Championship Event and my pocket aces had just lost to pocket queens, knocking me out on the bubble. It was EXCEPTIONALLY messed up because I was actually lulled into this false sense of safety. I was already visualizing myself at the final table, thinking about what I would wear. I mean, for sure I was going to make it to the money. I had plenty of chips and absolutely no intention of losing them. I remember saying to myself, 'I don't care what hand I get, the only two hands I'm playing are pocket aces or pocket kings and I might not even play the kings before this bubble bursts.' So, what do I look at next? Yea, you guessed it, fucking pocket aces. An extremely aggressive female raised the blinds yet again and I didn't try to play around with or bait with my pocket aces at all. I went all in pre-flop. The woman instantly called my shove. I felt EXTREMELY nervous. I looked away from the board as if I was hoping that if I didn't look, maybe nothing bad would happen. The pity-filled looks on the other ladies' faces and groans at the table told me everything I needed to know. I finally did look at the board, and confirmed the bad news. A fucked up queen had hit the flop and neither the turn nor river saved me from utter destruction. It felt as if someone punched me in the stomach. I'm out of the tournament!

Now, I have to say, what came next was probably one of the T.I.L.T.'iest moments I've ever had in my life. I stomped about the room thinking what, how, why, what the fuck!!!! I swore off poker. I never want to play that STUPID game again. I cried and screamed to the heavens, God WHY? Did I kill a puppy or something in a previous life? There was not one person who, or one thing that could, calm me down for *hours*.

If you've been playing poker long enough, you have probably experienced a loss like this (maybe not the 'strong reaction' so much; LOL.)

The severity of my reaction was in part due to my susceptibility of going into the deepest darkest depths of "Red Alert Brain."

There are many contributors to this type of strong reaction or reactivity. I will not go over all of those today, but will focus on the effect of past trauma. Personally, I come from a trauma background. Coming from a trauma background more often than not 'sentences' the traumatized to a lifetime of hypersensitivity. Basically, when there's enough danger for a long enough period of time introduced to a brain, the brain wires itself in ways that are meant to protect its host. Thus, hypervigilance, hyper-awareness,, strong reactivity, (i.e. other necessities to survive a war), is activated as part of the survival instinct. How does this impact living daily life?

Once we're no longer "fighting for our lives," the brain's perception that we need to be does not simply shut down; there is no on/off switch. So, what happens is we go about life often "over-reacting" to any negative stimuli (i.e. things that don't feel good.) Picture a spectrum of color with super light pink representing the slightest agitation and deep dark reds representing out of control rage. Depending on the extent of the trauma, without intensive self-work, the trauma victim is likely automatically pre-set at the lighter reds without any provocation.

Once provoked, and it may not take much provocation at all, RED ALERT (crisis) mode can be easily triggered. What we want, our goal here, is to regulate our emotions.

Hypersensitivity can also come from genetics, sensory or developmental disorders, neurological disorders, temperament.... Whatever the cause of hypersensitivity, it can seem impossible to manage

SUPER INTENSE emotions. But, never fear, I have found The Lafaya Way to be a helpful assistant in improving the ability to cope with emotional dysregulation. Following the 4 Core Steps, as mentioned above, activates your problem-solving mind. Activating your problem-solving mind aids in turning down the volume on emotional reactivity.

Cooling "Red Alert Brain" in action (using the sample bad beat story above):

Finding My Calm — Whoo, this is a toughee. This requires me to put on my therapist hat.
In the future, I could definitely work on avoiding personalization. Blaming my past life, God, the Universe, or some other force out there is never going to be good for emotional regulation. Initiating the deep breathing and progressive muscle relaxation exercises that I have been practicing for years now could also assist with calming my system. Knowing that I could go exercise all the negative energy out is also helpful to me. I especially love the boxing component to my exercise regimen; I look forward to getting the chance to hit something hard repeatedly.

Understanding the REAL Truth — Some REAL hard truths include:

Poker is a game of high variance; don't be surprised by losing when holding the dominating starter hand.

My tendency to have high emotional reactivity to upsetting events has more to do with my trauma history than it does the situation at hand. I am not in any real danger; I simply dislike the results I got.

I played the best hand, the best way I knew how; the results are out of my control and that is okay. I'll live to play another day.

Self-check-in (H.A.L.T.) — My being Hungry, Angry, Lonely and/or Tired could be amplifying my emotional reaction. Could a snack/meal, phoning a friend, or a nap help?

Responding in Alignment with My Truest Intentions —
It was definitely NOT my core goal to embarrass myself in front of the World Poker Tour staff and my fellow players by stomping around, punching into the air, talking to myself, while loudly whispering all kinds of obscenities.

With any loss, my core goal is to move into problem-solving mode (i.e. ask questions like 'Is there anything I could have done better?') As far as my play was concerned with that woman, my current answer is NOPE. I don't know anyone who would have folded pocket aces to an over-aggressive player's raise. I could, for sure, do loads of evaluation on my reaction and work on doing much better in the future. My core goal, reaction-wise, is to eventually be the classy player to congratulate, shake my opponent's hand, wish them well and mean it.

3-Rs: Recognizing My Small Step Improvements —
There are truly times in the past where I would have cussed out the other player, the dealer and the floor person and or any security personnel who tried to calm me down. My biggest urge would be to jump the table and beat the shit out of the player who sucked out on me. My stomping away loudly whispering obscenities, then going to find a place to cry and vent, is a vast improvement on who I was before that moment. Thinking about it now, where I am now has grown incrementally better than where I was at that moment. I can actually congratulate a player for beating me sometimes (this is definitely still a work in progress. LMAO)

Reinforcing Small Step Improvements
I'm actually doing that now, by speaking to, and feeling proud of, myself for my incremental improvements over time. Over time, my small improvements have turned into BIG improvements compared to where I started out. Other ways to reinforce may be to treat yourself to something nice, like a massage to congratulate yourself for your small step improvement.

Repeat — Recalibrate — Recycle — Keep working the steps!

Poker PTSD

Have you ever found yourself losing with the exact same hand so many times that you become leery of and maybe even physically repulsed by the idea of EVER playing that stupid hand again? I know that I have! I had a super bad run a couple of years back when I lost with pocket aces nine straight times within a period of two weeks. It got to the point where my heart would start to pound out of my chest, I'd have trouble breathing, and I would feel a little dizzy when I saw that STUPID hand. I would rather have been looking at deuce-seven than pocket aces. Was that HIGHLY illogical? YES, of course it was. So, what in the world was happening to me at that time??

I have taken to calling the phenomenon described above "Poker PTSD." The symptoms of it are an after-effect of severe Red Alert Brain moments, and nearly identical to PTSD. All of the feelings of the previous trauma comes back when you're faced with a similar situation based in a similar situation. For example, for war vets with PTSD, loud noises can startle them so much they can go into complete panic mode, even sometimes feeling like they're back in a previously dangerous situation, (i.e. under attack or heavy gunfire.) Poker players experiencing poker PTSD could look at a hand that has caused them harm multiple times in the past and be viscerally transported back to how they felt when traumatized by previous bad results. These PTSD moments can induce the following:

Alarm bells going off in our heads, Body feeling flush, Shortness of breath/Heaviness of chest, Muscles tensing, Uneasiness/Fidgeting, Heart racing, Feeling hot/Sweating, Feelings of pending doom, Expecting the worst to happen, Flashes of anger, Interruptions in strategically sound play, Folding a hand you are supposed to play, and even sending you into T.I.L.T.

Be intentional about using The Lafaya Way as an emotional regulation tool. The more you practice the steps, the better you'll get at calming, cooling, and/or bypassing Red Alert Brain, along with its cousin, Poker PTSD. T.I.LT.'ing will become less and less likely altogether.

Instincts, It Stinks

There are a few poker players out there who have the most gangster instinct I've ever encountered. Daniel Negreanu, one of the true OG players in the game, mastered a true understanding of the beginnings of GTO and had unmatched instincts to boot (true hybrid.) I would watch in amazement as he would call out the exact hands of his opponents without breaking a sweat.

A less well-known guy to the world, but very well known to me, with gangster ass instincts, is my husband, James. This guy has scary-like psychic abilities. When we first got together, I almost could swear that he was some type of warlock (man-witch) or something, because it seemed as if he was speaking and reacting to my thoughts and intentions more than what I was trying to put out there for him to pick up. He kind of drove me crazy. I couldn't get away with anything!

The most impressive play I have ever seen him do on the poker table just so happened to be a hand that involved him against me. He was holding pocket 8s and I was holding 10-J of clubs. The flop came, 8-9c-

Qs, giving him a set and me a straight and open-ended straight flush draw. The turn was the 8 of clubs, giving him four of a kind, (the third strongest hand possible in poker), and me the straight flush (the second strongest hand in poker.) He made a healthy bet, I thought in my head, 'Full house no good honey,' having no idea how REALLY strong his hand was, and I shoved. He thought for a good, long time, eventually folded his four of a kind face-up, and said to me, "Show them the straight flush." I was in COMPLETE SHOCK, revealed my hand and exclaimed, "If that was me, you would've had ALL my chips!" I still don't know to this day how in the world he was able to do that, but I have mad respect for his gangster instincts.

I actually have pretty good instincts myself. It is quite common for people who are raised in chronically dangerous environments to develop great intuition; strong instincts can become necessary for survival.

I have noticed that my rungood moments in poker tend to coincide with me being truly "tapped in," in the zone, or whatever you might call having very on-target instincts. During one of my rungood moments in a WPT Main Event hosted by Thunder Valley Casino, it almost felt as if I could do no wrong. Every decision I made was in the zone, trusting my instincts and I would come out on top, even with inferior starting hands to my opponents. I was flying high, easily making it to the final two tables.

And then, one split moment of temporary insanity cost me the tournament.

I was first to act with well over 30 big blinds. I raised with pocket nines. Before I made my raise, my higher mind (intuition) said, and I quote, "if anybody raises, I can just fold these." It folded around to the cutoff and chip leader at the table, who re-raised, 3x my raise. Insanity swept over my body, I completely forgot what intuition told me before I began the hand, and before I knew it, I was declaring, "ALL IN." The cutoff tanked for what felt like forever and finally made the right call with his pocket Jacks. Neither the flop, turn, nor river helped me and I was sent packing. What in the HELL was I thinking? I am truly floored by the way I squandered my first opportunity to take a real crack at getting my name on the Mike Sexton WPT Champions Cup and my first six figure payday. UGH!

I'd be remiss not to mention that my play was definitely not GTO approved either. I am a HUGE fan of GTO and in admiration of the robots who are able to live and breathe that shit. However, those of us who don't have five hours a day to study and run simulations sometimes have to rely on things like instincts or "it stinks" (i.e. I smell something fishy and I don't care what the rules are, I'm throwing this hand far, far away.)

Other Feelings

I have done PLENTY of things in the past to bring negative energy to myself and the game. I would do things like constantly proclaim that I am just unlucky, pout and feel sorry for myself after losing hands, criticize other players for their "donkey" play, blame the dealer or the tournament hosts, have full on meltdowns at the table, check messages on my phone and see something negative that affected my mood.

Best practices to improve your invisible energy levels at the poker table:

#1   Excellent self-care practices (Chapter "Self-Care is Important to Winning in Poker" has some suggestions for self-care)

#2 Turn devices off; don't get alerts that can upset you

#3 Work to see the positive in everything, especially in losses; since poker involves losing most of the time, think of losses as an opportunity to learn

#4 Last but not least, work The Lafaya Way 4 Core

Steps. They're AWESOME!

Connection to Step 2 of The Lafaya Way: Understand the "REAL" Truth

Another fantastic gift Jared gave me was this revelation. "Excitement and anxiety feel the same in the body." When I google searched Excitement/Anxiety similarities, this is what I found:

Physiological similarities: Both feelings can cause an elevated heart rate, sweating, and butterflies in the stomach. Both can also make you more alert and aware.

Emotional differences: Excitement is associated with joy while nervousness is associated with fear.

Interpretation: The difference between the two feelings is how you interpret them. For example, you might feel nervous before a tournament or poker session, but you might feel excited to have a chance to play the game you love and/or practice or show off some of the new strategies you have been learning.

Our goal is to learn what triggers these feelings in us and to interpret and respond to these feelings in a way that moves us toward a mindset that will bring positive vibes; thus supplying the invisible energy necessary (the "it" factor) to "be" a winner in the game of poker as well as in the game of life.

It is my belief that the grind of life prepares us

women for the grind of poker. We try to make the best decisions possible based on the sometimes very limited knowledge. Problem-solving on the regular is a definite requirement in life and in poker. We try to be proactive to stay ahead of life's challenges. But when required we make the pivots and adjustments necessary to try to gain as optimal results as possible. Multi-tasking is a way of life. We manage different personalities, being firm, soft, or whatever is necessary to get the job done at home and on the felt. Patience, an absolute must for tournament poker, is also definitely a requirement in our daily lives, especially when we have children. We tend to have what seems like an unlimited supply of mental strength and resilience. We have to practice keeping our cool and limiting our reactions constantly at home with husbands and children and at the poker table with assholes, pervs, and over-sized kids (baby-men.)

In conclusion: Is poker a woman's game? Hell yes ladies! We were made for this shit!

Lafaya Mitchell, Licensed Marriage and Family Therapist, Poker Player, Wife, and reluctant but happy mother of six, is on a mission to calm the effects of "Red Alert Brain." She aspires to share her life-changing philosophy, "The Lafaya Way" (created

in over 20 years of real life and professional experience) with the world.

She published three books in "The Lafaya Way" series and recently co-authored the #1 International bestseller, "SPEECHLESS: Giving the #voiceless a Voice."

Since "The Lafaya Way" is essentially the pathway to fostering living life in alignment with your truest intentions, Lafaya has found a way to apply her 4-step methodology used in therapy to battle T.I.L.T. (Temporary Interruption in Logical Thinking) in Poker.

Social Media Links:

Instagram: instagram.com/lafaya_way

Instagram.com/lafayawaypoker

Websites: lafayaway.com and lafayawaypoker.com

About The Author

Lafaya Mitchell, Lmft #47221

Author | Speaker | Trainer Lafaya Mitchell, LMFT, has over 20 years of experience with difficult to treat populations in the Mental Health Field; specializations include: Autism Spectrum Disorders and other moderate to severe social, emotional, and/or behavioral issues. After many prompts over the years by both parents and colleagues alike, she has captured in words the philosophy and methodology that has assisted her in offering hope and positive change to the lives of families with hyper-sensitive children who have failed in treatment often for years before being introduced to "The Lafaya Way" of responding.

She published three books in "The Lafaya Way" series and recently co-authored #1 International best seller, "SPEECHLESS: Giving the #voiceless a Voice"

Social Media Links:
Instagram: instagram.com/lafaya_way

Instagram.com/lafayawaypoker

Websites: lafayaway.com | lafayawaypoker.com

Books By This Author

Speechless: Giving The #Voiceless A Voice

Lafaya Mitchell is co-author of this, the best-selling book of all 16 books in Lonnee Rey's series of anthologies:

From non-verbal to loquacious, living or legendary, everyone has something vital to say which adds to the richness of our lives in myriad ways.

In this short read, you will meet different examples of being speechless: A beauty pageant family that doesn't accept alternate life choices; an introvert that became a Toastmaster; a poker player who turned pain into healing, two men who chose to die before their voices faded, a daughter's love/hate story that inspired her to create a legacy of better communication with her children, and a best friend who passed but whose messages of love, family and forgiveness will live on.